Through The Narrow Gate

by

Arthur E. Sidner

Library of Congress Control Number (LCCN): 9781966647980

ISBN(e-Book): 979-8-218-80373-5
ISBN(PB): 978-1-966647-98-0

Published by:
Authors Publishing House
178 Broadway, 3rd Floor, #1343
New York, NY 10001, USA

Main Line: (855) 624-0155
Email: support@authorspublishinghouse.com

For information, contact:

Arthur E. Sidner

10055 Braddock Road   Apt. 118

Fairfax, Virginia 22032

E-mail: aesidner@gmail.com

Table of Contents

Preface

"And the Lord God commanded the man, 'You may freely eat of every tree of the garden; but of the tree of the knowledge of good and evil you shall not eat, for in the day that you eat of it you shall die.'" -- Genesis 2:15-17

When the first humans rebelled against God and ate of the tree of the knowledge of good and evil, they died spiritually and lost the quality of inner life that God intended us to have. Jesus Christ came to restore this lost quality of inner life.

Disciples of Jesus Christ are those who are more than simply believers, but are actively seeking to become just like Jesus. I am writing this book for disciples of Jesus Christ to assist us to experience more consistently, the quality of inner life that Jesus promised that we would have while we were on this earth.

"I came that they may have life and have it abundantly." -- John 10:10

I have been a disciple of Jesus Christ for over 60 years, and I have experienced this quality of inner life for much of that time but not all the time. I will describe my experience with the metaphor used by Jesus in Matthew 7:13,14:

"'Enter through the narrow gate; for the gate is wide and the road is easy that leads to destruction, and there are many who take it. For the gate is narrow and the road is hard that leads to life, and there are few who find it.'"

The narrow gate is our relationship with Jesus himself, and the hard road is the course of life that God has marked out for us to follow during our time on earth.

I entered through the narrow gate over 60 years ago and set out on the hard road, but sometimes I turn back, slip and fall off the road, try to take a shortcut off the road, stop going forward, receive bad directions and leave the road for a time, and so forth.

I am writing for those who have entered through the narrow gate and begun their journey on the hard road leading to the quality of inner life that Jesus wants us to experience.

I intend for this book to be used like a spiritual travel guide, to help all of us disciples to stay on the hard road more consistently.

At the end of the book, I present a vision of what could happen if more disciples reach a level of spiritual maturity where they become God's coworkers to help God carry out his plans for the world.

This book will not be easy to understand and assumes a general familiarity with the holy scriptures [quotes are from the New Revised Standard Version, Anglicized (NRSVA) unless otherwise noted].

Introduction
Life and Death

In Apostle John's gospel, he makes the following statement about what he and his fellow disciples observed during the three years they followed Jesus on earth:

". . . in him was life, and the life was the light of all people." -- John 1:4

John felt that the **quality of inner life** that they saw in Jesus was in fact, the life that all human beings were meant to experience, what all human beings longed for.

". . . this life was revealed, and we have seen it and testify to it, and declare to you the eternal life that was with the Father and was revealed to us" -- 1 John 1:2

In this book I will use the term "eternal life" to mean the quality of inner life that John observed in Jesus, i.e., the life of Jesus.

"'For God so loved the world that he gave his only Son, so that everyone who believes in him may not perish but may have eternal life.'"
-- John 3:16

In his letter to the Colossians, Apostle Paul discusses the profound mystery that this life of Jesus could be imparted (inside of them) to those who believe in Him.

". . . the mystery that has been hidden throughout the ages and generations but has now been revealed to his saints. To them God chose to make known . . . this mystery, which is Christ in you, the hope of glory."
-- Colossians 1:27

Jesus' use of the terms "life and death"

In John's gospel, Jesus uses the terms "life" and "death" in an unusual way, to describe a person's inner experience.

"'Very truly, I tell you, the hour is coming, and is now here, when the dead will hear the voice of the Son of God, and those who hear will live.'"
-- John 5:25

Here, Jesus is referring to people who are biologically alive, but spiritually dead.

Paul's use of the terms, "life and death"

Paul uses the concepts of life and death in a similar manner in Ephesians 2:1-2 and Romans 7:9-10.

"You were dead through the trespasses and sins in which you once lived, following the course of this world, following the ruler of the power of the air, the spirit that is now at work among those who are disobedient."

"I was once alive apart from the law, but when the commandment came, sin revived, and I died"

I will use the term, "spiritually dead" to refer to an inner experience (motivation and attitudes) characterized by:

- Not having a conversational relationship with God (you don't speak to God and God doesn't speaks to you) and not wanting to please God
- Not knowing your spiritual purpose or that your life has any eternal significance
- Being in bondage to the sin in the members of your body (characterized by fear, doubt, guilt, anxiety and an inharmonious relationship with the rest of creation)
- Being subject to the dominating influence of evil spirits

In the above passage in John 5, Jesus says that persons who were spiritually dead might "hear" his voice and become spiritually alive. This process of becoming spiritually alive is called being born from above in John 3:3.

I will use the term "spiritually alive" to refer to an inner experience characterized by:

- Having a conversational relationship with God (you speak to God and God speaks to you in his own time and manner) and wanting to please God
- Knowing that you have a spiritual purpose and your life has eternal significance
- Being able to respond to situations with the character of Jesus Christ (characterized by love, joy, peace, and a harmonious relationship with the rest of creation)

- Not being subject to the dominating influence of evil spirits

The Great Complication – two sources of inner experience

Paul taught that believers in Jesus Christ and indwelt by the Holy Spirit, have two sources of inner experience dwelling in them at the same time. In this book, I will use the terms "flesh" and "Spirit," to describe these sources of inner experience.

Paul's use of the term, "flesh"

In Paul's letters, he uses the term, "flesh" over 30 times to describe one source of your inner experience [your natural, created life + sin].

While we were living in the **flesh***, our sinful passions, aroused by the law, were at work in our members to bear fruit for death.*

For I know that nothing good dwells within me, that is, in my **flesh***. I can will what is right, but I cannot do it.*

Thanks be to God through Jesus Christ our Lord! So then, with my mind I am a slave to the law of God, but with my **flesh** *I am a slave to the law of sin.*

Paul's use of the term "Spirit"

In Paul's letters, he uses the term, "Spirit" over 25 times to describe another source of your inner experience [your uncreated {eternal} spiritual life], if you have received this life from Jesus. **It is the Spirit that produces the motivation and character of Jesus Christ inside of us.**

But now we are discharged from the law, dead to that which held us captive, so that we are slaves not under the old written code but in the new life of the **Spirit***.*

For those who live according to the flesh set their minds on the things of the flesh, but those who live according to the **Spirit** *set their minds on the things of the* **Spirit***.*

IN SUMMARY

True believers in Jesus Christ, indwelt by the Holy Spirit, have two sources of inner experience, i.e. the flesh and the Spirit. At any moment in time, one of these sources is the dominant influence upon their personality. Paul also speaks of our situation as having a treasure (the Spirit) hidden inside of an ordinary clay vessel (the flesh). This makes it clear that the treasure is from God and not from us.

"But we have this treasure in clay jars, so that it may be made clear that this extraordinary power belongs to God and does not come from us."
-- 2 Corinthians 4:7

Another way to think about these two sources of inner experience is that:

The flesh is the life we were created with, the life we were born into this world with. Jesus calls this being born of the flesh or being born of water.

The Spirit is the life that always was, uncreated, imparted to us when we believe. Jesus calls this being born of the Spirit.

Believers in Jesus Christ are influenced by both of these life sources and their inner experiences are a mixture of flesh and Spirit. Paul vividly describes this in Galatians 5.

I am writing this book to help believers reduce the influence of the flesh and increase the influence of the Spirit in their everyday lives.

Chapter 1

A new way of relating to God

The old covenant

Even though Jesus Christ was born and raised in a Jewish community, which included practicing the Jewish religion of his day (the "old covenant" between God and his people), it is clear that Jesus came to initiate a new way of relating to God. He revealed this truth gradually to those he met during his three years of earthly ministry.

To a Samaritan woman he met at a well:

"Jesus said to her, 'Woman, believe me, the hour is coming when you will worship the Father neither on this mountain nor in Jerusalem. But the hour is coming, and is now here, when the true worshippers will worship the Father in spirit and truth, for the Father seeks such as these to worship him.'" -- John 4:21,23

To his Jewish disciples at a supper, the night before he died:

"Then he took a loaf of bread, and when he had given thanks, he broke it and gave it to them, saying, 'This is my body, which is given for you. Do this in remembrance of me.' And he did the same with the cup after supper, saying, 'This cup that is poured out for you is the new covenant in my blood.'" -- Luke 22:19,20

1

The new covenant

This "new covenant" that Jesus referred to, was a new way of relating to God which was first promised long ago by the prophet Jeremiah:

"The days are surely coming, says the Lord, when I will make a new covenant with the house of Israel and the house of Judah. It will not be like the covenant that I made with their ancestors when I took them by the hand to bring them out of the land of Egypt—a covenant that they broke, though I was their husband, says the Lord. But this is the covenant that I will make with the house of Israel after those days, says the Lord: I will put my law within them, and I will write it on their hearts; and I will be their God, and they shall be my people. No longer shall they teach one another, or say to each other, 'Know the Lord', for they shall all know me, from the least of them to the greatest, says the Lord; for I will forgive their iniquity, and remember their sin no more." -- Jeremiah 31:31-34

This new covenant was necessary because humans could not keep their part of the old covenant. This new covenant became possible after Jesus' propitiatory sacrifice paid for all the sins committed under the old covenant, thus fulfilling its requirements. This new covenant was formally instituted after Jesus was crucified, raised from the dead and ascended into heaven.

One of Jesus' first acts under this new covenant was to send the Holy Spirit to dwell in and with his disciples on the Day of Pentecost. The presence of the Holy Spirit makes it possible for a person to know God inside of themselves and to live in union with God.

Whether or not this possibility is consistently realized in your personality depends upon your faith. For purposes of this book, I will define biblical faith as *believing in your heart what God says and acting as if what you believe is true.* (See Appendix I.)

". . . if you confess with your lips that Jesus is Lord and believe in your heart that God raised him from the dead, you will be saved. For one believes with the heart and so is justified, and one confesses with the mouth and so is saved." -- Romans 10:9-10

An initial word about "faith"

"Now faith is the assurance of things hoped for, the conviction of things not seen. Indeed, by faith our ancestors received approval. By faith we understand that the worlds were prepared by the word of God, so that what is seen was made from things that are not visible." -- Hebrews 11:1-3

The writer of Hebrews speaks of "faith" as a way to relate to realities that we cannot see with our natural eyes, a way to understand things that we cannot prove. Faith, for the believer, is like proof, to the scientist.

"Faith" according to Apostle Paul vs. Apostle James

The assignment given to Apostle Paul by Jesus Christ from heaven, was to bring about the obedience of faith among the Gentiles.

". . . through whom we have received grace and apostleship to bring about the obedience of faith among all the Gentiles for the sake of his name," -- Romans 1:5

This was a different kind of obedience from the way most Jews were taught under the old covenant. Paul was criticized by his Jewish brethren for teaching this kind of obedience to the Gentiles. This teaching became a major source of conflict between the church in Jerusalem, which was predominately Jewish, and the predominately Gentile churches taught by Paul.

Apostle James uses different language than Paul but they both speak about the same reality. James speaks about biblical faith in this way:

"So faith by itself, if it has no works, is dead. But someone will say, 'You have faith and I have works.' Show me your faith without works, and I by my works will show you my faith. "

"Was not our ancestor Abraham justified by works when he offered his son Isaac on the altar? You see that faith was active along with his works, and faith was brought to completion by the works."

"For just as the body without the spirit is dead, so faith without works is also dead." -- James 2:17. 21, 22, 26

For James, faith consists of what you believe and how you act based on that belief.

Paul speaks about biblical faith in this way:

"For what does the scripture say? 'Abraham believed God, and it was reckoned to him as righteousness.' Now to one who works, wages are not reckoned as a gift but as something due. But to one who without works

trusts him who justifies the ungodly, such faith is reckoned as
righteousness." -- Romans 4:3-5

On the surface, it looks like the teachings of these two apostles are in conflict. But if you look beyond the surface, you see that only their emphases are different.

James wants to see "works of faith." James is concerned with people who say they believe but display no evidence of that belief.

Paul is concerned with people who try to earn God's favor by doing "charitable works" or by "keeping the law with their own abilities" rather than by trusting God's grace to come to them without their earning it, empowering them to do what God requires.

For both James and Paul, faith is a heart conviction which always results in action based on that belief.

The individual nature of biblical faith

The well-known examples of faith mentioned in Hebrews 11, show that biblical faith is not just a set of beliefs that can be passed down from one generation to another. This faith is an individual inner conviction. Different people have different capacities for this faith and the results of this faith in the lives of those living under the new covenant will differ. Paul teaches in Romans 12:3 that God has assigned to each of us a certain measure of faith, which we should live out without comparing ourselves to others or expecting others to have the same faith as ours.

"The faith that you have, have as your own conviction before God."
-- Romans 14:22

IN SUMMARY

Jesus emphasized a way of relating to God by faith **(the new covenant)** which was an extension of the way Abraham related to God.

Over 400 years after the death of Abraham, when Moses led the nation of Israel out of Egypt, he instituted a way for his people to relate to God which scripture calls **the old covenant**, characterized by obedience to written laws.

Despite this, there were always people during this period who lived by faith, such as King David.

"So also, David speaks of the blessedness of those to whom God reckons righteousness irrespective of works:" -- Romans 4:6

When Jesus came to earth, it was difficult for those Jewish disciples of Jesus who were used to **the old covenant**, to comprehend **the new covenant**. Remember when Jesus said:

"And no one, after drinking old wine, wants new, because he says, 'The old is better.'" -- Luke 5:39

Under **the old covenant**, God told his people what he required of them, and they were expected to fulfill those requirements using their own abilities. The old covenant is about obedience.

Under the new covenant, God expects his people to trust him to give them the power to fulfill his requirements, even though they can't fulfill them using their own abilities. The new covenant is about faith.

Chapter 2

Relating to the Jesus who Is now

"John, to the seven churches that are in Asia:

Grace and peace to you from the one who is and was and is coming, and from the seven spirits that are before God's throne, and from Jesus Christ—the faithful witness, the firstborn from among the dead, and the ruler of the kings of the earth.

To the one who loves us and freed us from our sins by his blood, who made us a kingdom, priests to his God and Father—to him be glory and power forever and always. Amen." -- Revelation 1:4-6

In the above passage, Apostle John writes to seven churches and reminds them who they are relating to, the Jesus who is now – who is alive as a man with a glorified body sitting at the right hand of God in the heavenly realm, waiting until his enemies are made a footstool of his feet. **Jesus wants to interact with us from heaven now.**

Since we cannot see Jesus now, we must relate to Jesus by faith, the way Jesus related to God the Father when he was on earth (i.e. Jesus could not see the Father). This is also the way Apostle Paul related to Jesus (i.e. Paul could not see Jesus). From this relationship we will receive all the power that Jesus promised his disciples that they would receive.

The proper role of the scriptures

"All scripture is inspired by God and is useful for teaching, for reproof, for correction, and for training in righteousness, so that everyone who belongs to God may be proficient, equipped for every good work."

-- 2 Timothy 3:16

I believe that the scriptures are a collection of writings in various literary styles with God speaking in union with a human voice (or a human voice speaking in union with God), sometimes without the human understanding what is spoken. The personality and feelings of the writers often show through. They are not a word-for-word dictation where the human writer is only a secretary.

The scriptures are the channel through which we learn about Jesus and the life that he has for us, and a major channel through which God speaks to us, but the scriptures themselves are not that life. As Jesus said to the Pharisees in John 5:39:

"'You search the scriptures because you think that in them you have eternal life; and it is they that testify on my behalf. Yet you refuse to come to me to have life.'"

The "spirit" of the scriptures vs. the "letter" of the scriptures

The old covenant was about conformity to the letter of the scripture, but the new covenant instituted by Jesus requires that we focus on the spirit of the scripture, not just the letter. As Paul says in his second letter to the Corinthians:

"You yourselves are our letter, written on our hearts, to be known and read by all; and you show that you are a letter of Christ, prepared by us, written not with ink but with the Spirit of the living God, not on tablets of stone but on tablets of human hearts.

. . . our competence is from God, who has made us competent to be ministers of a new covenant, not of letter but of spirit; for the letter kills, but the Spirit gives life." -- 2 Corinthians 1:2-6

The experience of life that we seek is only to be found in the person, Jesus Christ, not in the scriptures by themselves.

Relating to Jesus by faith involves our speaking with our heavenly Father (Jesus said we should ask the Father), verbally confessing what we believe and acting as if what we believe is true, and waiting for God to speak to us and act on our behalf in his own time and manner.

The old covenant was about obeying the written word, but the new covenant is more about relating to a person in an intimate, loving relationship.

"Blessed be the God and Father of our Lord Jesus Christ, who has blessed us in Christ with every spiritual blessing in the heavenly places, just as he chose us in Christ before the foundation of the world to be holy and blameless before him in love." -- Ephesians 1:3-4

"Jesus answered him, 'Those who love me will keep my word, and my Father will love them, and we will come to them and make our home with them." -- John 14:23

In this book, I will give examples of how I have related to Jesus (See Appendix II) and suggestions for how you might relate to him, but ultimately, you must relate to him according to your own personality and situation. There are no formulas for relating to Jesus that work for everybody.

IN SUMMARY

As we see in the gospel record, Jesus' life as a man was centered around his relationship with his heavenly Father and his Father's purposes. Jesus found that his own needs were met as he focused on fulfilling his Father's purposes. This is why we human beings were created.

"Jesus said to them, 'My food is to do the will of him who sent me and to complete his work." -- John 4:34

"But strive first for the kingdom of God and his righteousness, and all these things will be given to you as well." -- Matthew 6:33

After we human beings rebelled against God (in the Garden of Eden and repeated throughout history), we tried unsuccessfully to center our lives around ourselves and our human purposes. We succumbed to the devil's temptation to become like God.

Through the gift of the Holy Spirit, we can now know God intimately, inside ourselves, and fulfill the purpose for which we were created.

The scriptures were given to help us relate to the one who is life, not to be life in themselves.

Chapter 3

The ministry of reconciliation

"So, if anyone is in Christ, there is a new creation: everything old has passed away; see, everything has become new! All this is from God, who reconciled us to himself through Christ, and has given us the ministry of reconciliation; that is, in Christ God was reconciling the world to himself, not counting their trespasses against them, and entrusting the message of reconciliation to us." -- 2 Corinthians 5:17-19

In this present age, God is about restoring his relationship with human beings (which was lost when humankind rebelled against God). He is not about condemning human beings for their sins. This is exemplified by the ascended Jesus calling Saul of Tarsus (a man who violently opposed those who called on the name of Jesus) to be his apostle to the Gentiles.

"You have heard, no doubt, of my earlier life in Judaism. I was violently persecuting the church of God and was trying to destroy it."
-- Galatians 1:13

"I am grateful to Christ Jesus our Lord, who has strengthened me, because he judged me faithful and appointed me to his service, even though I was formerly a blasphemer, a persecutor, and a man of violence. But I received mercy because I had acted ignorantly in unbelief, and the grace of our Lord overflowed for me with the faith and love that are in

Christ Jesus. The saying is sure and worthy of full acceptance, that Christ Jesus came into the world to save sinners—of whom I am the foremost."
-- 1 Timothy 1:12-15

Grace and truth vs. Law

"The law indeed was given through Moses; grace and truth came through Jesus Christ." -- John 1:17

Among religious figures in biblical history, Jesus' impact is compared to that of Moses. But unlike Moses, who mostly emphasized what God required of his people (law), Jesus exposed what humans were really like, including their inner motives, but gave those who believed him, the grace to be what they were originally intended by the Creator to be.

I think of grace as the spiritual energy that comes to us from God that enables us to do what God requires of us. (This is different from mercy, which refers to God not judging us when we don't do what is required.)

Heart attitudes vs. Outward behavior

Jesus focused more on our inner heart attitudes than our outward behavior because outward behavior flows from heart attitudes.

"'But I say to you that everyone who looks at a woman with lust has already committed adultery with her in his heart.'" -- Matthew 5:28

"'Either make the tree good, and its fruit good; or make the tree bad, and its fruit bad; for the tree is known by its fruit. You brood of vipers! How can you speak good things, when you are evil? For out of the abundance

of the heart the mouth speaks. The good person brings good things out of a good treasure, and the evil person brings evil things out of an evil treasure.'" -- Matthew 12:33-35

Jesus talked about us becoming good on the inside, not just trying to be good on the outside, like the Pharisees who opposed Jesus. This is why the new covenant can work because we will not be trying to act contrary to what we really feel inside.

". . . blotting out the handwriting of ordinances that was against us, which was contrary to us." -- Colossians 2:14

Conviction vs. Condemnation

Even though God is not now condemning human beings for their sins and their ignorance of him, he is convicting them of their sins, commanding them to repent and announcing the coming judgment.

"'Indeed, God did not send the Son into the world to condemn the world, but in order that the world might be saved through him." -- John 3:17

"While God has overlooked the times of human ignorance, now he commands all people everywhere to repent, because he has fixed a day on which he will have the world judged in righteousness by a man whom he has appointed, and of this he has given assurance to all by raising him from the dead.'" -- Acts 17:31-32

Because Jesus has paid the penalty for our sins, we can respond to conviction without fear, by acknowledging our sins, knowing that God will forgive us.

"If we confess our sins, he who is faithful and just will forgive us our sins and cleanse us from all unrighteousness." -- 1 John 1:9

God's method of proclamation

God has chosen to use the simple proclamation of the news about Jesus Christ (who he is and what he has done) as the means of saving human beings.

"For since, in the wisdom of God, the world did not know God through wisdom, God decided, through the foolishness of our proclamation, to save those who believe." -- 1 Corinthians 1:21

This has gone on for the last two thousand years and today, in the twenty-first century, God's people can be found in nearly every nation on earth.

Salt and light

Part of God's strategy is to use his people in every human culture as salt (preserving that culture from moral decay) and light (showing that culture what human life is supposed to be).

"'You are the salt of the earth; but if salt has lost its taste, how can its saltiness be restored? It is no longer good for anything but is thrown out and trampled underfoot.'"

" 'You are the light of the world. A city built on a hill cannot be hidden. . .
In the same way, let your light shine before others, so that they may see
your good works and give glory to your Father in heaven."
-- Matthew 5:13-14

This strategy requires that God's people be transformed in order to become spiritually mature.

The imperative of maturity

"And all of us, with unveiled faces, seeing the glory of the Lord as though
reflected in a mirror, are being transformed into the same image from one
degree of glory to another; for this comes from the Lord, the Spirit."
-- 2 Corinthians 3:18

The inner transformation that Jesus promises to produce in us takes some time, analogous to the fact that human bodies take some time to mature. This transformation is not automatic but requires that we cooperate with the Holy Spirit as he convicts us of sin and tries to get us to agree with him and repent.

"to equip the saints for the work of ministry, for building up the body of
Christ, until all of us come to the unity of the faith and of the knowledge of
the Son of God, to maturity, to the measure of the full stature of Christ."
-- Ephesians 4:12-13

Unfortunately, many believers do not cooperate with the Holy Spirit and fail to mature, such as the believers at Corinth in the time of Apostle Paul.

"And so, brothers and sisters, I could not speak to you as spiritual people, but rather as people of the flesh, as infants in Christ." -- 1 Corinthians 3:1

When the people of God do not mature spiritually and they fail to be a credible witness for God to a particular culture, leading to the moral decline of that culture, God may discipline his people by means of persecution from the surrounding culture.

IN SUMMARY

Before the creation of the world, God purposed to have humankind living with him in a loving relationship. God anticipated that humankind would rebel against him and become alienated from him. In this present age, God is about restoring his relationship with human beings.

Over two thousand years ago, God sent his Son into the world to show what human life was supposed to be, to foreshadow and announce the kingdom of God, and to die as a propitiatory sacrifice for the sins of the world.

Before he left earth he committed this ministry of reconciliation to his followers.

Disciples of Jesus Christ have the great privilege of being God's coworkers in this ministry during this present era, before Jesus returns to earth to judge the world, but this requires that they become spiritually mature.

Chapter 4

We must travel the hard road in "newness of life"

The biggest obstacle to overcome along the hard road is our attachment to our old life. Our "flesh," **the old life we were born with, is not capable of making the trip.** This is a truth that takes most of us a long time to learn. After all, our old life has taken us this far, what could be so bad about it? It seems that only by trying to live faithfully in our own strength, and failing over and over again, do we learn:

"For I know that nothing good dwells within me, that is, in my flesh. I can will what is right, but I cannot do it." -- Romans 7:18

Jesus alluded to this problem of our old life when he said,

"Then Jesus told his disciples, 'If any want to become my followers, let them deny themselves and take up their cross and follow me. For those who want to save their life will lose it, and those who lose their life for my sake will find it." -- Matthew 16:24-25

The problem of sin in our flesh

Usually, when we first become disciples, we assume that God wants to use what we think of as the good qualities of our "flesh," for his service. That was surely the case with Apostle Paul who could say,

"If anyone else has reason to be confident in the flesh, I have more: circumcised on the eighth day, a member of the people of Israel, of the tribe of Benjamin, a Hebrew born of Hebrews; as to the law, a Pharisee; as to zeal, a persecutor of the church; as to righteousness under the law, blameless." -- Philippians 3:4-6

But our problem is that we are unaware of the sin in our "flesh" that expresses itself through our personality in ways that we typically attribute to others instead of ourselves. Jesus saw this very clearly when he said,

" 'Woe to you, scribes and Pharisees, hypocrites! For you are like whitewashed tombs, which on the outside look beautiful, but inside they are full of the bones of the dead and of all kinds of filth.' "
-- Matthew 23:27

Apostle Paul taught in Romans 2:1:

"Therefore, you have no excuse, whoever you are, when you judge others; for in passing judgement on another you condemn yourself, because you, the judge, are doing the very same things."

We think of sin as being about our behavior, but Jesus saw the source of sin as our heart attitudes (i.e. murder comes from hate). I believe this is why Jesus and Paul taught disciples not to be judgmental of others.

"Why do you see the speck in your neighbor's eye, but do not notice the log in your own eye? Or how can you say to your neighbor, "Let me take the speck out of your eye", while the log is in your own eye? You

hypocrite, first take the log out of your own eye, and then you will see
clearly to take the speck out of your neighbor's eye." -- Matthew 7:3-5

A special hint

Usually, when we feel very judgmental about something we see in others, it is because we have the same heart attitude in ourselves, which we have not acknowledged but projected onto others. Remember God holds us responsible for our heart attitudes whether or not we have expressed them through our behavior. This was the case in the story of the woman caught in adultery who was brought to Jesus by scribes and Pharisees. They pointed out to Jesus that the law said she should be stoned, and Jesus said,

"'Let anyone among you who is without sin be the first to throw a stone at
her.'" -- John 8:7

None of the men who brought the woman to Jesus would throw the first stone.

Sin is part of who we are, not just what we do.

I have come to think of sin like an alien virus (passed on genetically to each generation) that exists within my old natural life, which I am not conscious of, and which is usually dormant, but under certain circumstances can awaken and take over my personality. Paul taught in Romans 7:8-10:

"But sin seized the opportunity and used this commandment to produce all
kinds of desires in me. Sin is dead without the Law. I used to be alive

without the Law, but when the commandment came sin sprang to life, and I died."

Only after becoming truly aware of our sin, especially our sinful heart attitudes (for most people, this takes a number of years), are we ready to accept God's solution to our problem. This is why Paul cautions against putting young believers in positions of authority.

> NOTE: It is important to point out that Jesus had no sin in his flesh. Even though he was fully human, with all the limitations and weaknesses of a human, he was not genetically related to Joseph because Mary conceived him by the Holy Spirit before she was ever intimate with Joseph. Jesus was not exactly like the rest of us. Therefore, we cannot expect our inner experience to be perfect like it was in Jesus.
>
> *"For we do not have a high priest who is unable to sympathize with our weaknesses, but we have one who in every respect has been tested as we are, yet without sin." -- Hebrews 4:15*

Our death – God's solution to the problem of sin in our flesh

". . . All of us died to sin. How can we still live in it? Or don't you know that all who were baptized into Christ Jesus were baptized into his death? Therefore, we were buried together with him through baptism into his death, so that just as Christ was raised from the dead through the glory of the Father, we too can walk in newness of life." -- Romans 6:1-4

This **newness of life** is a new set of motivations and attitudes like those of Jesus Christ, produced in us by the Holy Spirit. They show up in our Christ-like responses to life situations, not just our conscious behavior (which we can control with our will). Paul teaches more of the details about this in Romans chapters 5, 6 and 7. Just as we were all in our first progenitor Adam, when he sinned, God placed us in our second progenitor Christ, when he died on the cross, such that:

- When Christ was crucified, we were crucified.
- When Christ was buried, we were buried.
- When Christ was raised from the dead to a new life, we were raised from the dead to a new life.

This is hard to understand but our task is to believe this and act as if it were true. The implications of this are life changing.

1. **Put to death your old life – what we must learn in order to walk in this newness of life.** Start by verbally acknowledging that you died to sin.

    "I have been crucified with Christ and I no longer live, but Christ lives in me." -- Galatians 2:19b-20a

    "Put to death, therefore, whatever in you is earthly: fornication, impurity, passion, evil desire, and greed (which is idolatry)."
    -- Colossians 3:5

2. **Learn to disidentify with sin.** If you have the life of Christ inside you, this is your *true life* and sin is simply something that resides in your *old life*, in your flesh, in the members of your body. If you become aware of some sinful attitude rising within you, acknowledge this specific attitude as sin, but disidentify with it by stating:

". . . it is no longer I that do it, but sin that dwells within me. For I know that nothing good dwells within me, that is, in my flesh. I can will what is right, but I cannot do it. For I do not do the good I want, but the evil I do not want is what I do. Now if I do what I do not want, it is no longer I that do it, but sin that dwells within me."
-- Romans 7:17-20

As the Holy Spirit convicts you of other sinful attitudes, confess them as sin and repeat the above procedure.

"This *(name the specific attitude)* is not I, but the sin that dwells within me."

3. **Give up your rights.** Our old life is self-centered. If your old life has died, you have no more personal rights, such as the right to be treated with respect, the right to have things your own way, etc. When you find yourself reacting negatively to the way someone, or life circumstances, have violated your perceived rights, try stating:

"I die to my right to have things go my way."

In my experience, this is the most difficult part of putting to death our old life.

4. Continually confess your new life in Christ.

> *"The life I now live in the flesh I live by faith in the Son of God, who loved me and gave himself for me." -- Galatians 2:20b*

As we learn to do this repeatedly over time, sin will gradually lose its grip on us, and our experience of this **newness of life** will gradually increase and deepen as we mature from spiritual babes to spiritual adults.

The righteousness of God that comes by faith

Paul is our example of one who put this into practice and learned to live in this newness of life.

Paul also called this **newness of life** that God produced within him, "the righteousness of God" in contrast to a righteousness that he could produce on his own.

Toward the end of his life on earth, Paul had successfully completed his journey on the hard road that leads to life and he could say,

> *"Yet whatever gains I had, these I have come to regard as loss because of Christ. More than that, I regard everything as loss because of the surpassing value of knowing Christ Jesus my Lord. For his sake I have suffered the loss of all things, and I regard them as rubbish, in order that I may gain Christ and be found in him, not having a righteousness of my*

own that comes from the law, but one that comes through faith in Christ,

the righteousness from God based on faith." -- Philippians 3:7-9

IN SUMMARY

The new covenant instituted by Jesus works because we do not have to walk in our old life, which contains sin, to try and fulfill God's requirements. We can learn to walk in **newness of life,** which is the life of Christ, that does not contain sin.

Those who have been born of God do not sin, because God's seed abides

in them; they cannot sin, because they have been born of God."

-- 1 John 3:9

However, we must be willing to die to our old life before the new life of Christ, produced by the Holy Spirit, can emerge and be expressed through our personality. We can die to our old life by acknowledging the sin in our own attitudes when we are convicted by the Holy Spirit, disidentifying with sin ("this is not I"), giving up our rights, and confessing by faith that the life of Christ is our new "I." Our mantra should be **"no confidence in flesh"** (Philippians 3:3).

As we do this repeatedly, the influence of the flesh upon our personality will gradually diminish and the influence of the Spirit will gradually increase.

Chapter 5

The necessity of childlike faith

"He called a child, whom he put among them, and said, 'Truly I tell you, unless you change and become like children, you will never enter the kingdom of heaven." -- Matthew 18:3

I believe one of the major issues preventing many believers in Jesus Christ from experiencing the benefits of the life of faith (especially in Western cultures) is the natural cynicism we acquire as we grow from children to adults. A child who has a positive relationship with their father will likely accept what their father says, regardless of whether they fully understand it but as the child grows into adulthood, this becomes less so.

The life of faith requires that we believe in our hearts, many things which appear impossible to our intellect. Most of us either consciously or unconsciously subscribe to the motto that *seeing is believing*. Thus, when Abram's wife Sarai heard that she would have a natural birth child at the age of 90, her response was to laugh. On the contrary, when the teenager Mary was told she would give birth to a child before she ever had intimate relationships with a man, she replied,

"'Here am I, the servant of the Lord; let it be with me according to your word.' "-- Luke 1:38

For the life of faith, the motto is *believing is seeing,* implying that seeing comes after believing (See Appendix I-D).

God's word to us flows from his character and since God does not lie and nothing is impossible to him, when God says something, we must believe that it is true no matter how impossible it might look to us.

" 'Whoever has accepted his testimony has certified this, that God is true."
-- John 3:33

"Those who do not believe in God have made him a liar by not believing in the testimony that God has given concerning his Son." -- 1 John 5:10

Thus, our faith has more to do with our perception of God's character than our understanding of what he tells us.

We are Abraham's spiritual children if we exhibit a faith like his.

Apostle Paul uses Abraham as our model for faith.

"The purpose was to make him the ancestor of all who believe . . . who follow the example of the faith that our ancestor Abraham had before he was circumcised." -- Romans 4:11-12

There are several aspects of our faith that are like Abraham's faith which he exhibited over his long life of 175 years (see Genesis 12 – 25):

- We believe that God justifies the ungodly.
- We believe that God can bring life out of death.
- We believe that God can call things into existence that do not exist.

- We believe that God can deliver what he has promised us, no matter what the outer circumstances become.

Abraham believed that God could bring life out of his and Sarah's "dead" bodies, and he believed that if he killed his son Isaac, as God asked him to do, God could bring Isaac back from the dead.

We must believe that God raised the man Jesus from the dead (2 Timothy 2:8) and that God can and will bring forth the life of Christ out of our spiritually dead bodies if we ask and believe him to do this.

IN SUMMARY

Our progress along the hard road that leads to life depends primarily on the quality of our faith. When it comes to relating to the invisible God, we must let go of the cynicism that we acquire as we grow up in a modern sophisticated culture and relate to God like simple trusting children with a loving father.

The patriarch Abraham exhibited a faith like this and we are asked to model our faith after his faith.

Chapter 6

God is always working

"But Jesus answered them, 'My Father is still working, and I also am working." -- Matthew 18:3

Ever since the sin of humanity separated us from God, God has been working to restore that relationship. Because God's ways are different from ours, it has been difficult for us to perceive how he is working. Jesus, however, was very alert to what God was doing, both short term and long term.

"He has made known to us the mystery of his will, according to his good pleasure that he set forth in Christ, as a plan for the fullness of time, to gather up all things in him, things in heaven and things on earth. In Christ we have also obtained an inheritance, having been destined according to the purpose of him who accomplishes all things according to his counsel and will," -- Ephesians 1:9-11

God's long-term plans focus on his Son, not on us. We are blessed to be included in the working out of God's plans.

"Blessed be the God and Father of our Lord Jesus Christ, who has blessed us in Christ with every spiritual blessing in the heavenly places, just as he chose us in Christ before the foundation of the world to be holy and blameless before him in love." -- Ephesians 1:1-2

God is at work inside of us disciples of Jesus Christ.

To make us holy and blameless, God works inside of us by his Spirit, with our cooperation, to replace our self-centeredness with the motivation and character of Jesus Christ.

". . . for it is God who is at work in you, enabling you both to will and to work for his good pleasure." -- Philippians 2:13

"For we are His workmanship, created in Christ Jesus for good works, which God prepared beforehand that we should walk in them."
-- Ephesians 2:10

God is at work in the world.

In the world, God's short-term plans include using his people to make himself known to all nations. He does this by leading his people to behave and do things that can only be explained by the fact that God is with them.

"And he said to them, 'Go into all the world and proclaim the good news to the whole creation." -- Mark 16:15

"But if all prophesy, an unbeliever or outsider who enters is reproved by all and called to account by all. After the secrets of the unbeliever's heart are disclosed, that person will bow down before God and worship him, declaring, 'God is really among you.'" -- 1 Corinthians 14:24-25

God is at work behind the scenes.

Even when we cannot observe any evidence of God working, we can be confident that he is working behind the scenes both inside of us and in the world, to make things work out toward his purposes.

"We know that all things work together for good for those who love God, who are called according to his purpose." -- Romans 8:28

God wants us to be his coworkers.

As we mature and become coworkers with God, we can ask and believe God to show us what he is doing so we can cooperate with him just like Jesus and Abraham.

"'The Father loves the Son and shows him all that he himself is doing;'"
-- John 5:20

"The Lord said, 'Shall I hide from Abraham what I am about to do,'"
-- Genesis 18:17

We work in union with God – we are not self-sufficient.

"'Rabbi, we know that you are a teacher who has come from God; for no one can do these signs that you do apart from the presence of God.'"
-- John 3:1-2

The above comments directed to Jesus are from Nicodemus, a leading teacher of the Jews. Specifically, the comments refer to the signs which Jesus was performing. The apostles and other disciples performed similar signs after they received the Holy Spirit. The important issue is that both

Jesus and the apostles learned to live and work in union with God, not as self-sufficient beings.

Jesus said (and the apostles could also say),

". . . 'Very truly, I tell you, the Son can do nothing on his own, but only what he sees the Father doing; for whatever the Father does, the Son does likewise.'" -- John 5:19

"'Do you not believe that I am in the Father and the Father is in me? The words that I say to you I do not speak on my own; but the Father who dwells in me does his works.'" -- John 14:9

Most believers think that Jesus performed signs and wonders because he was the divine Son of God, but I think it is more likely (since he emptied himself of his divine attributes) that Jesus performed these signs as a human being in union with the Holy Spirit, just like his disciples did and just like we can do.

"Let the same mind be in you that was in Christ Jesus, who, though he was in the form of God, did not regard equality with God as something to be exploited, but emptied himself, taking the form of a slave, being born in human likeness. And being found in human form, he humbled himself and became obedient to the point of death—even death on a cross."
-- Philippians 2:5-8

"Very truly, I tell you, the one who believes in me will also do the works that I do and, in fact, will do greater works than these, because I am going to the Father." -- John 14:12

Apostle Peter worked in union with God when he healed a lame man on his way to the temple in Acts 3. When people tried to credit Peter with this miraculous sign, Peter said:

" 'You, Israelites, why do you wonder at this, or why do you stare at us, as though by our own power or piety we had made him walk?' " -- Acts 3:12

Moses was able to take on the impossible task of freeing the Israelites from Egypt because God promised to work along with him.

"But Moses said to God, 'Who am I that I should go to Pharaoh, and bring the Israelites out of Egypt?' He said, 'I will be with you;"
-- Exodus 3:11-12

IN SUMMARY

God is always at work inside of us and in the world, to advance his purposes.

Inside of us, God changes us by his Spirit into the image of Christ, as we learn to acknowledge and repent of the sin he shows us and believe him to replace our fleshly motivation and character with the motivation and character of Jesus Christ.

In the world, God works by joining himself to human beings and working through them (through their prayers and actions). We become his coworkers by discerning what he is doing, joining him in his work, and by faith, working consciously in union with him.

Chapter 7

God is not like us

"For my thoughts are not your thoughts nor are your ways my ways, says the Lord.

For as the heavens are higher than the earth, so are my ways higher than your ways and my thoughts than your thoughts." -- Isaiah 55:8-9

It is critical to our faith that we have right expectations about God. One of the things that makes our life with God difficult is that we expect God to behave the way we would behave if we were God and we get angry or disappointed when God does not behave that way. Too often, we approach God as if we were on the same level of being as God. We forget that God is not a human person and is on a much higher level of being than we are.

"God is not a human being, that he should lie,
or a mortal, that he should change his mind.
Has he promised, and will he not do it?
Has he spoken, and will he not fulfil it?" -- Numbers 23:19

God does not respond to us in the time frame and manner that we would expect from other human beings. His purposes do not center around us. We must learn to orient our lives around God and his purposes, not vice versa. This will require that we change our way of thinking.

"Do not be conformed to this world, but be transformed by the renewing of your minds, so that you may discern what is the will of God—what is good and acceptable and perfect." -- Romans 12:2

The lives of Moses and the patriarchs Abraham and Joseph, illustrate that God's sense of timing and his manner of working are quite different from ours.

When Moses grew up and wanted to help liberate his people, he had to wait 40 years until God sent him back to Egypt to accomplish this task.

When Abraham was 85 years old, God promised him that he would have many descendants, but he had to wait another 15 years before he had his first child, Isaac.

When Joseph got a dream that he would be in authority over his brothers, he had to wait nearly 20 years before circumstances in Egypt made it possible for God to raise him up to a position of authority.

One of the important things we must acknowledge is that God is sovereign. He is the creator of everything and there is no greater authority than God. He has the right to do anything that he wants with his creation.

"God who made the world and everything in it, he who is Lord of heaven and earth, does not live in shrines made by human hands," -- Acts 17:24

"Will what is molded say to the one who molds it, 'Why have you made me like this?' Has the potter no right over the clay, to make out of the same

lump one object for special use and another for ordinary use?"

-- Romans 9:20-21

Having right expectations of God, helps to keep us from the paralyzing doubts that Satan plants in our hearts when God does not behave the way we think he should.

"He (Satan) said to the woman, 'Did God say, "You shall not eat from any tree in the garden"?'" -- Genesis 3:1

"But ask in faith, never doubting, . . . for the doubter, being double-minded and unstable in every way, must not expect to receive anything from the Lord." -- James 1:6-8

IN SUMMARY

Even though God wants to have an intimate conversational relationship with us and wants to be our friend, he is not a human friend. He is on a much higher level of being than us and we must take that into consideration when it comes to our expectations of how God will interact with us.

God's thoughts and ways of doing things are higher than ours.

Chapter 8

Standing against spiritual evil - avoiding the devil's deception

"For our struggle is not against enemies of blood and flesh, but against the rulers, against the authorities, against the cosmic powers of this present darkness, against the spiritual forces of evil in the heavenly places." -- Ephesians 6:12

There are unseen spiritual forces that are opposing what God is trying to do on earth. We are familiar with the visible evil forces at work on the earth and the human weapons used to destroy them, such as physical force, manipulation, law, etc. On the other hand, destroying invisible spiritual forces of evil and defending ourselves against them, requires that we employ spiritual weapons.

"Finally, be strong in the Lord and in the strength of his power. Put on the whole armor of God, so that you may be able to stand against the wiles of the devil." -- Ephesians 6:11

". . . for the weapons of our warfare are not merely human, but they have divine power to destroy strongholds. We destroy arguments and every proud obstacle raised up against the knowledge of God, and we take every thought captive to obey Christ." -- 2 Corinthians 10:4-5

In this book I will focus on the attempts of these evil spiritual forces to deceive God's people. First, I direct your attention to an incident in the time of King David where Satan put the thought in David to call for a census of the men of Israel, something that was expressly forbidden by God. This disobedience resulted in God sending a plague that killed thousands.

"Satan stood up against Israel, and incited David to count the people of Israel." -- 1 Chronicles 21:1

Second, there is an incident in the time of King Ahab of Israel where God allowed this wicked king to be deceived by putting a lying spirit in Ahab's prophets to direct him to engage in a battle that would result in his death.

". . . until a spirit came forward and stood before the Lord, saying, "I will entice him." The Lord asked him, "How?" He replied, "I will go out and be a lying spirit in the mouth of all his prophets." Then the Lord said, "You are to entice him, and you shall succeed; go out and do it." So you see, the Lord has put a lying spirit in the mouth of these your prophets; the Lord has decreed disaster for you.'" -- 2 Chronicles 18:20-22

Third, listen to Apostle Paul's admonition to Timothy to be careful about putting young believers in positions of leadership because they might become conceited.

"He must not be a recent convert, or he may be puffed up with conceit and fall into the condemnation of the devil. Moreover, he must be well thought

of by outsiders, so that he may not fall into disgrace and the snare of the devil." -- 1 Timothy 3:6-7

In each of these examples, it was the unjudged sinful attitudes of God's people in leadership (pride, conceit, hate, fear, etc.) that made them susceptible to the devil's lies and cause harm to come to God's people. This is why it is so important to **become aware of our sinful heart attitudes and repent of them**, lest we be deceived by evil spiritual forces.

IN SUMMARY

We are in a spiritual war. We live in a world where evil spiritual forces oppose the work of God. The most common tactic used by the devil is to deceive the minds of human beings, lying to them.

When our sinful heart attitudes (pride, conceit, jealousy, anger, etc.) are motivating us to act, the devil is able to plant thoughts in our minds that are in harmony with these motivations and deceive us into acting in ways contrary to God's will.

We must put on God's spiritual armor (truth, the righteousness that comes from God, preparation for proclaiming the gospel, faith, knowledge of salvation, knowledge of the scriptures) to avoid being deceived by the devil.

Chapter 9

Who to listen to

One of the features of modern society is the democratization of public platforms. Whereas at one time, only a few authority figures had access to speak to the entire public, today, through social media, anyone can speak to everyone. There are so many voices speaking that it is hard to know who to listen to.

Most of us end up listening only to those who reinforce our own opinions about what is, or what should be, going on. Another issue is that, through Artificial Intelligence (AI), it is possible to show an image and mimic the voice of someone we are familiar with and make that image say anything we want it to say. How do we know what is true, especially when it comes to those who claim to speak for God?

"Then Jesus answered them, 'My teaching is not mine but his who sent me. Anyone who resolves to do the will of God will know whether the teaching is from God or whether I am speaking on my own. Those who speak on their own seek their own glory; but the one who seeks the glory of him who sent him is true, and there is nothing false in him."
-- John 7:16-18

Jesus was questioned by the religious leaders of his day regarding the authenticity of his message. Jesus' advice was simple: Anyone who sincerely wanted to do God's will rather than his own will, would know whether his message was authentic or not. This makes perfect sense. If you want to do only what God wants, God is going to make sure you are not in doubt about what that is. We can trust God, but the question is, can God trust us?

A word of caution to those who would speak for God

In the above passage, Jesus speaks of the motives of those who claim to speak for God without God having sent them. In our time, prestige, positional power and money can easily corrupt people into claiming to speak for God to develop a following. Such was the case for many of those religious leaders who questioned Jesus in Matthew 21:23.

"When he entered the temple, the chief priests and the elders of the people came to him as he was teaching, and said, 'By what authority are you doing these things, and who gave you this authority?'

The religious leaders were upset because Jesus was not under the authority of an earthly person or institution. Jesus' authority came from God, who is the one who sent Jesus to do and speak what he did. We should listen to those who are sent from God and those who claim to speak for God should continually monitor their own motives to ensure that they are sent from God.

"Whoever speaks must do so as one speaking the very words of God;"

-- 1 Peter 4:11

The importance of revelation

There are so many opinions about what the scriptures mean. Scholars claim to know because of the exhaustiveness of their studying but Paul reminds us that only the Spirit of God truly knows what God intends and **the only way we can truly know is if God reveals this directly to our spirits.** Our intellect alone is not adequate for such discernment. Paul's knowledge of God came through revelation, not his superior intellect.

"These things God has revealed to us through the Spirit; for the Spirit searches everything, even the depths of God. For what human being knows what is truly human except the human spirit that is within? So also no one comprehends what is truly God's except the Spirit of God. Now we have received not the spirit of the world, but the Spirit that is from God, so that we may understand the gifts bestowed on us by God."
-- 1 Corinthians 1:10-12

Jesus said that the pure in heart would see God (Matthew 5:8), not those who are brilliant in intellect. A pure heart is a heart that is morally like the Creator. Thus, in matters that pertain to God, **it is our heart motives that are the critical issue, not the brilliance of our intellect.**

Paul reminds us in 1 Corinthians 1:20-21:

"Where is the one who is wise? Where is the scribe? Where is the debater of this age? Has not God made foolish the wisdom of the world? For since, in the wisdom of God, the world did not know God through wisdom,

God decided, through the foolishness of our proclamation, to save those who believe."

Jesus spoke about being wary of false prophets.

" 'Beware of false prophets, who come to you in sheep's clothing but inwardly are ravenous wolves. You will know them by their fruits . . . Thus, you will know them by their fruits." -- Matthew 7:15-20

IN SUMMARY

The modern world is flooded with information by people with all kinds of inner motives, who claim to speak for God. This makes it difficult for disciples, seeking to learn what God wants, to know who to listen to.

The most critical issues in knowing who to listen to, are the purity of our own heart motives and the actual results in the lives of those who claim to speak for God.

Chapter 10

A word about learning

"'A disciple is not above the teacher, nor a slave above the master; it is enough for the disciple to be like the teacher, and the slave like the master.'" -- Matthew 10:24-25

Before he began his teaching ministry at the age of thirty, Jesus spent many years **learning:**

- from the elders in the temple in Jerusalem and in his local synagogue,
- from the scriptures,
- from his own experiences

In this context, I am using the term "learning" to mean acquiring the skill to live by faith, like Jesus, Abraham, Moses, David, and Paul.

To make progress along the hard road that leads to life, we must become good **learners.** Jesus is the author and perfecter of living by faith. We can only please God if we **learn** to live by faith like Jesus did when he was on earth.

". . . without faith it is impossible to please God" -- Hebrews 11:6

Research and my own experience have confirmed that effective learners must employ diverse learning practices. To truly **learn**, we cannot simply read or listen to concepts.

". . . for everyone who lives on milk, being still an infant, is unskilled in the word of righteousness. But solid food is for the mature, for those whose faculties have been trained by practice to distinguish good from evil. -- Hebrews 5:13-14

Scripture itself contains diverse types of literature designed to accommodate different learning practices.

"All scripture is inspired by God and is useful for teaching, for reproof, for correction, and for training in righteousness, so that everyone who belongs to God may be proficient, equipped for every good work."
-- 2 Timothy 3:16-17

1. **Learning sometimes begins by reflecting on our negative experience.** When our spiritual experience has not been satisfactory, we can ask God questions and seek to learn concepts that explain our experience or predict what might lead to better experiences. An example might be when Jesus' disciples were unable to cast a demon out of a child and they asked Jesus, 'Why could we not cast it out?'

2. **This book primarily teaches abstract concepts.** After reflecting on our experience, we can study concepts that might enhance our faith experience. Most of the concepts in this book are based on the writings of Apostle Paul who was well-taught in both the Hebrew scriptures and Greek literature.

3. **It is not enough to understand concepts intellectually. These concepts must be confirmed by running our own faith experiments.** We learn best if we can try out concepts to see if they work out in our own lives. Appendix II contains my testimony of faith experiments that have worked for me. You should design your own faith experiments that fit your personality. Trial and error are okay.

4. **Our experiences confirm whether or not the concepts work.**

To get the most benefit from this book, do not simply read it once or twice but read it repeatedly, **using these 4 Learning Practices** until your experience matches your expectations.

IN SUMMARY

Being an effective disciple requires being a good **learner.** Jesus did not just teach his disciples abstract concepts in a classroom setting. He engaged them in the normal activities of life, using a variety of learning practices and he sent them out on their own to practice what they had learned from him.

We can make progress along the hard road that leads to life if we employ all 4 Learning Practices mentioned in this book.

Epilogue

The promise of spiritual maturity

As we mature spiritually, we disciples will experience that quality of inner life that we long for and fulfill that purpose for which we were originally created. Only then can we become capable of cooperating with God so God can work through us, *using his power working through human beings* to make himself known to the world.

God does not want to coerce human beings but rather, secure their willing cooperation from a motive of love, as he did with Abraham, Moses, King David, Jesus Christ, and Apostle Paul.

The superior plans of God

In the scriptures, we see that God has plans for the benefit of his creation which he intends to achieve through human beings, like he did with Moses and Jesus. God's plans for blessing the world, *using his power working through human beings,* are far superior to any of the plans that we humans produce to help God, using our abilities alone. It is my hope that more disciples of Jesus Christ become his coworkers and learn to cooperate with God as he works out his plans.

I believe that the near-term fate of the world may rest upon our doing so. Let us keep moving forward along the hard road that leads to life.

Appendix I

Illustrations about walking by faith

"For one believes with the heart and so is justified, and one confesses with the mouth and so is saved." -- Romans 10:10

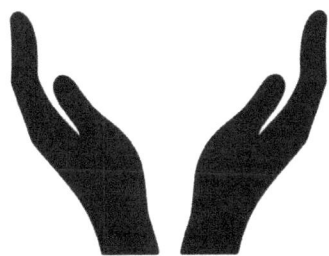

A. We reach up to God and trust that God will fill our hands

We reach up to God by believing in our hearts what God has said, verbally confessing what God has said, thanking God that this is true, and acting as if God has done what he said, trusting that we will experience the result in God's time and manner.

B. We place the forms and trust God to pour the concrete

We place the forms by believing in our hearts what God has said, verbally confessing what God has said, thanking God that this is true, and acting as if God has done what he said, trusting that God will pour the concrete and that we will experience the result in God's time and manner.

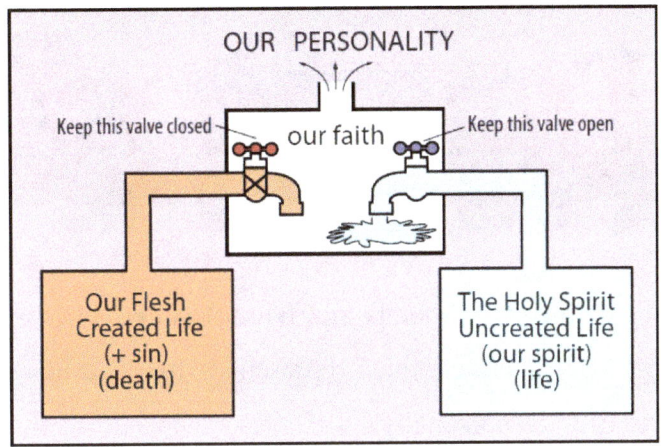

OUR PERSONALITY

our faith

Keep this valve closed

Keep this valve open

Our Flesh
Created Life
(+ sin)
(death)

The Holy Spirit
Uncreated Life
(our spirit)
(life)

C. We open the Holy Spirit valve and keep the flesh valve closed

We open the Holy Spirit valve by believing in our hearts that God has given us the Holy Spirit, verbally confessing that God has given us the Holy Spirit, thanking God that he has done so, and acting as if God has given us the Holy Spirit, trusting that we will experience the Holy Spirit in God's time and manner.

We close the flesh valve by verbally acknowledging as sin, specific motivations and attitudes contrary to the life of Jesus that we are experiencing, believing in our hearts and confessing verbally that we have been crucified with Christ and no longer live, and are thus dead to sin.

We keep the Holy Spirit valve open by believing in our hearts that we are alive to God in Christ Jesus, and that we now live by the faith of the Son of God who loved us and gave himself for us, trusting that we will experience the life of Christ (his motivations and attitudes) in God's time and manner.

D. We believe God's facts and trust that experience will follow

First comes the engine, which represents what God has said, either in the scriptures or to us personally.

Next comes the passenger car, which represents our faith. We believe what God has said with our hearts and verbally confess what God has said, thanking God that this is true, and acting as if God has done what he said.

Finally (can be a short time or a long time after faith) comes the caboose, which represents our actual experience, either inside ourselves or in external circumstances.

Appendix II

My testimony

In the summer of 1963, in Saint Paul, Minnesota, I first encountered a group of teenagers who displayed a quality of inner experience that I had never seen before. They spoke about God as if they knew him and they were passionately following God's purpose for their lives. I wanted this quality of inner experience for myself.

I was 22 years old, had been baptized as a baby and confirmed as a young teenager but I had no conversational relationship with God. During that summer I was convicted by the Holy Spirit that I was a sinner and needed a personal savior. I verbally acknowledged my sin, asked Jesus to come into my heart, and committed my life to him.

I expected to feel something inside me to indicate that I now had eternal life, but I felt nothing different. I was not certain that I had a relationship with Jesus and when people asked me if I was "saved" I could not answer in the affirmative.

I came across John 5:24 where Jesus said:

"Very truly, I tell you, anyone who hears my word and believes him who sent me has eternal life, and does not come under judgement, but has passed from death to life."

I knew that I believed what God said about Jesus and based on this verse, I concluded that I did have eternal life. After that, when people asked me if I was "saved" I would say "yes." I continued to make this verbal confession and after a short time, I realized that I did feel something different inside and I have never doubted my salvation since that time.

I began to grow in faith, particularly through studying the scriptures and participating in church and various spiritual activities with other believers but I struggled to overcome old sinful habits. I was still in bondage to sin.

In the early 1970s, I heard the testimony of people who spoke of overcoming sin in their lives by applying what Apostle Paul taught in Romans 5–7 about dying to self. I began to apply this teaching by verbally confessing that I was crucified with Christ and sin had no more authority over me, that I died to my right to have things go my way, and that I now lived by the faith of the Son of God who loved me and gave himself for me. As I repeatedly applied this teaching, I noticed that I gradually became free from bondage to my old sinful habits and my responses to situations became more Christ-like.

In the late 1970s, I met believers in the Charismatic Renewal who had rediscovered the power of the Holy Spirit to speak in unknown tongues, lay hands on people to heal their sickness, prophesy and cast out demons, etc.

I wanted to experience this power, so I reaffirmed that I had received the Holy Spirit, citing this verse:

"'If you then, who are evil, know how to give good gifts to your children, how much more will the heavenly Father give the Holy Spirit to those who ask him!'" -- Luke 11:13

I reasoned that since the Holy Spirit is the author of languages, I had the ability to speak in any language that the Holy Spirit chose to give me. I began to practice speaking gibberish and after continuing this for several days, I noticed a pattern in this gibberish that I had not made up – first syllables, then words, then phrases, then an intelligible language that I could not translate. For the last 47 years I have used this unknown language in my private prayer life and found that it edifies me. In addition, I have experienced prophetic visions, and I have laid hands on sick people and seen them healed.

In the 1980s, I experienced a mid-life crisis and benefited by learning to share how I felt with a therapist, who taught me to write how I was feeling in a journal. I began to practice writing in my journal as if I were talking to God and listen for God to talk back to me in the form of persisting thoughts that would arise in me. If I felt God was speaking to me, I would write what I felt God said in my journal in a dialogue form. In this way, I have continued a dialogue with God in my journals for the last 40 years and this has helped me maintain and grow in my relationship with him.

Over the years, I have often relapsed into living by the flesh instead of the Spirit and found myself slipping back into bondage to my old sinful habits and feeling distant from God, strained in my relationship with the

Holy Spirit who lives within me. As Apostle Paul described so colorfully in Romans 7:11, sin has deceived me and killed me spiritually.

God's mercy has always drawn me back to him as he did with King David, even when David sinned grievously. At such times, I have been able to confess my sin and begin again to apply Paul's teaching about death to self and God has graciously brought me back to life spiritually. God is still showing me sin in my flesh that I need to confess as he works to complete the image of Christ in me.

Now, in my 85th year in 2025, I look back on my failures with some regret, like the patriarch Jacob in Genesis 47:9, but I also look forward with expectation that God can still use me in his work in the world, and I press on to finish my race of faith.

-- Art Sidner